神农溪上的纤夫

主编 周超

TRACKERS OF SHEN NONG XI

By Zhou Chao

目录

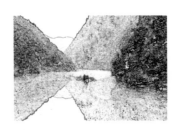

CONTENTS

神农溪

神农溪位于长江三峡巫峡与西陵峡之间的湖北省巴东县境内，因发源于神农架南坡故名。神农溪全长60公里，沿途接纳了大小十七条溪涧，坡降相对落差2700米，山峦相续，逶迤绵延，两岸绝壁夹峙，山岩多成80－90度。在陡峭的岩壁上有悬棺、古栈道遗迹清晰可见。幽深的绵竹峡中溪涧最窄处不及5米，神农溪年平均日流量20立方米／秒，神农溪经西壤口汇入长江巫峡段。

SHEN NONG XI

Shen Nong Xi is situated in Badong County, Hubei Province, running between Wu Strait and Xiling Strait, both are parts of Three-Strait of Changjiang River. As it is born in the south slope of Shen Nong Jia, it is called Shen Nong Xi. Shen Nong Xi is 60km long, along the way 17 brooks and gullies join it. It has 2,700m fall, running cross mountains and valleys, with cliffs of 80-90 gradient on both banks. On the steep cliffs, coffins and plank road are built, they are recognized as wonders of human kind. Mianzhu Gully's throat, the most narrow section is 5m wide. Shen Nong Xi joins Wu Strait at Xirangkou, at flow of 20m³/s.

SHEN NONG XI

1988年8月4日，在神农溪畔观看"神农溪首漂式"的当地群

神农溪于1988年正式对外开放，1988年8月4日举行的"神农溪首漂仪式"十分隆重。当年，以国家旅游局局长刘毅为首的首漂式来宾云集巴东山城。在首漂式当天，闻讯赶来看热闹的神农溪两岸的老百姓，从四面八方聚集在神农溪两岸，盛况空前。巴东县城的码头上也是人如潮涌，鞭炮声响彻云霄，小城里忙得热火朝天，如同节日一般！

In 1988, Shen Nong Xi was officially opened to the public, and held First Drift Ceremony on Aug. 4, 1988. On that day, Liu Yi, president of National Tourism Administration presented the ceremony, the people from both banks of Shen Nong Xi, they witnesses the pageant. The Badong Dock was crowded by spectators, firecrackers light up the sky above Shen Nong Xi, the small city spent a unforgettable festival.

神农峡

神农溪景区共分四个峡段，有"神农峡"、"绵竹峡"、"鹦鹉峡"、"龙昌峡"，四个峡都各具特色，集险、秀、雄之美于一体，妙趣天成。

罗坪故州　Luoping Old City

神农峡处于神农溪漂流游中第一个峡段，峡段全长25公里，由岩棺峡和破石峡组成。神农溪漂流集散地罗坪在神农峡的中段,罗坪古称罗坪故州。如今的罗坪已形成一个大湖泊，水面宽广清澈妩媚，这里是开展各种水上娱乐项目的理想地。神农峡历史悠久，峡中古遗迹随处可见，有九孔岩、石罅类岩棺、九层楼等多处人文景观，岩棺峡属于宽谷、半峡地貌，另据特色。行径峡中有人在画中游的畅快感觉，在这个峡段游客将体验纤夫拉纤的全过程。

九孔岩 *Nine-Hole Rock*

Shen Nong Xi consists of four gullies, i.e. Shen Nong Gully, Mianzhu Gully, Parrot Gully, Longchang Gully, all of them are works of god, dangerous, scenic and grand.

岩棺 *Hanging coffin*

Shen Nong Gully, the first section of Shen Nong Xi, is 25km long, consisting of Yanguan Gully and Poshi Gully. The drift camp is built in Luoping, the former Ancient Luoping City, the waist of Shen Nong Gully. Today's Luoping has a big lake, clean and vast, it is idea to hold various water amusement programs. Shen Nong Gully has a long history, and countless heritages, cultural landscapes, e.g. Jiukongyan, Shixia Cliff Coffin, Nine-floor Tower. Yangua Gully is a wide valley, also a semi strait, distinct in landforms. Roam in the gully, you may feel as if you have entered a fairyland, where some naked men are tracking boats on the beach.

绵竹峡一线天
Mianzhu A Ray of Sunlight

綿竹峡 MIANZHU GORGE

　　绵竹峡是注入神农溪的一条支流，长四公里，两岸相峙，有一线天、蟒蛇出山、野人伸掌、半边街、大鹏展翅等栩栩如生的自然和人文景观。沿岸还有许多古人类居住过的大小洞穴二十多处。每逢雨过天晴时，绵竹峡里的溪面上会形成一层薄雾，使峡谷景观更添神秘色彩，置身其中令人回味无穷。一线天景观更是叫绝，两岸之间只有4-5米，相峙直上，成90度。天空成了一条狭窄的长线，谓之一线天。

逆水行舟　Sailing Upstream

MIANZHU GORGE

胜景天成　Beautiful nature scenery of shennong Stream

Mianzhu Gully, 4km long, is a branch of Shen Nong Xi. The cliffs on both banks hold each other in the sky. Here you will see a lot of natural and humanistic views such as A Ray of Sunlight, Boa Out, Wild Man, A Side of Street, Hawk Winging. On both sides are over twenty caves of pithecanthropes. In rainy weather, when sun breaks clouds, Mianzhu Gully look as if in a misty cloth, everything look mystery. A Ray of Sunlight is a wonder of the world, it's only 4-5m wide, the cliffs from both sides are perpendicular to each other. Only a line of sky can be seen, that's why it is called A Ray of Sunlight.

蟒蛇出山 Snake Out

峭壁长廊 Steep Gallery

在绵竹峡中闯滩的船老大　Captain of Mianzhu Gully

由于绵竹峡里滩多水急，水情凶险，一般在绵竹峡漂流时，船老大总是亲自披挂上阵，在船前操舵，不敢怠慢。你看那强悍的身躯，有力的臂膀和那古铜色的肌肤，能使你虽置身险情中却不觉惊恐，虽初入此境却安然处之。仿佛船上的纤夫就是自己的保护神，神农溪纤夫的魅力慑服众多探寻而来的人们。给人留下难忘的印象。

Mianzhu Gully, characterized by numerous hidden shoals and rush flows, the drifting is dangerous. Drifting in Mianzhu Gully must be piloted by the captain, he dares not release the nerves for a second till the journey ends. The captain has mighty muscle, powerful arms and bronze-coloured skin, guarded by such a hero, you will feel easy in any dangerous situations, even though for the first time you come here. The trackers on the bank are your guards, they are impressively left in every tourist' memory.

绵竹峡另一大奇观，钟乳石群落。在幽深的峡谷之中满布着各种形态的钟乳石，有的形似巨蟒，有的象展翅的飞鹰，有的似饮水的猴群，你尽管发挥自己的想象力在石群中搜寻探索为它们命名。

峡中荡舟 Rowing through Strait

MIANZHU GORGE

绵竹峡中的钟乳石
Stalactite of Mianzhu Gully

垂手可及的钟乳石
Stalactite at Hand

大家说说这块石头象什么？
What is the stone like?

Stalactite is another wonder of Mianzhu Gully. They are grotesque in shape, growing in tranquil valleys. Some look like snake, some look like hawk, some look like monkeys, you can give them any name you like best.

14

龙昌峡雨情　Rain of Longchang Gully

雨中的纤夫　Trackers in Rain

龙王庙前的香客　Pilgrims of Dragon Temple

岩棺峡里的漂流　Drifting through Yanguan Gully

16

鹦鹉峡

YINGWU GORGE

鹦鹉峡全长7.5公里，重峦叠嶂、山秀水美，两岸灌木丛生。峡中恬静幽雅，鸟语花香，树丛中猴群嬉戏，不时还能看见山崖上野生黄羊伫立跳跃，獐麂穿行，红腹锦鸡也扑腾着翅膀在杂草中寻觅食物。在鹦鹉峡里更有气势宏大的燕子阡大溶洞景观，燕子阡溶洞里常年栖息着好几万只短嘴金丝燕，当你走近洞口仰天望去，穿行与洞天之间的金丝燕密密麻麻十分壮观。峡中的岩壁上古栈道留下的石孔随处可见，相传太平天国时期刘体纯将军曾在此征战。

野生动物黄麂 Genus Muntiacus

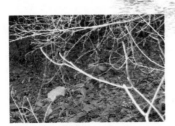

草丛中的红腹锦鸡
Chrysolophus Pictus In Grassland

灵气十足的雾鼠 Fog Mouse

燕子阡大溶洞 Yanziqian Karst Cave

鹦鹉峡滴翠 Green Parrot Gully

YINGWU GORGE

Parrot Gully, 7.5km long, is embraced by scenic mountains, with bush in both banks. It is like a tranquil garden, birds are singing, flowers are blooming, monkeys are playing game in woods, if you are lucky, you will see wild yellow sheep, genus Muntiacus, Chrysolophus pictus on the grassland. Parrot Gully also treasures grand Yanziqian Karst Cave, where there living thousands of fuciphaga. Looking up at the gate of the cave, you will see flocks of fuciphaga flying in the sky. The stone holes left in the plank road is also a surprise to you, it is said that Liu Chunjun, a general of Taiping Dynasty ever fought battles here.

常年活动在鹦鹉峡中的猴群　Monkey living in Parrot Gully

在鹦鹉峡中，有一座海拔1000米高的山峰"高视岩"，登上高视岩眺望神农溪，眼见得烟云飞逝，溪流蜿蜒，气势磅礴。高视岩上雄鹰翱翔，透过葱郁灌木丛山羊群在满山盛开的杜鹃花中觅食。

巴东山羊　Badong Goat

神农溪上的最高点 [高视岩] Summit of Shen Nong Xi

猫头鹰 Owl

Gaoshiyan, a 1000-meter-high mountain in Parrot Gully, is the best sight-seeing stage to overlook total views of Shen Nong Xi, looking from here, flying clouds, zigzag brooks are all in a picture. Above your head hawks are flying, across the bush, sheep are seeking food in the azalea clumps.

叶子坝漂流 Yeziba Drifting

　　在鹦鹉峡与龙昌峡之间，有一个土家村落叫龙船河村。村里的男人们大多都在神农溪上当纤夫，风吹日晒挣钱养家，而村上的女人们则在家中生儿育女、耕田养猪。每天傍晚村妇们会拎着竹篓带上香喷喷的饭菜到码头上去迎接自己的丈夫，当纤夫们回到码头会立刻从老婆手中接过竹篓，一边谈笑着一边寻着河床上干净点的卵石坐下，狼吞虎咽般的享受着老婆为自己烹饪的美味。接下来的便是该回家的唱着小曲回了各自的家，第二天一早有活干的还要把船往上游码头拉……

土家阿妹 A Girl of Tujia Nationality

Between Parrot Gully and Longchang Gully, there is a village of Tujia Nationality called Longchuanhe Village. In the village, men tracks boats in Shen Nong Xi, women stay at home, take care of children, breed stocks and do farming. At dusk, the women come to the dock, with delicious dishes in bracket. Here boatmen will take a break, sit on the clean screes, enjoy the supper in the setting sun. At night, some boatmen may go home, some may continue their risky journey.

神农溪上纯朴的民族风情　Folk of Shen Nong Xi

　　上世纪八十年代中期，一首歌曲《纤夫的爱》风靡大江南北，全国上下老小都能哼唱几句，可是没有几个人知道这首歌的MTV外景是在神农溪上实拍的。也不知靠这首歌走红的歌手尹相杰和于文华是否还能记得，神农溪！这块风水宝地。什么时候再到神农溪来做一回纤夫，扮一回土家妹子，如今的神农溪可是大变模样了。

In the mid 1980s, a pop song Love of Boatmen ever prevailed the whole country, even everybody can sing this song, but few people know this MTV is taken in Shen Nong Xi, the stars Yin Xiangjie and Yu Wenhua, are famous for this song, do they still remember Shen Nong Xi? If they come back to Shen Nong Xi, show again the love of boatmen, they may find, great changes have taken place in Shen Nong

神农溪上的纤夫
Trackers of Shen Nong Xi

龙昌峡雄姿 Panorama of Longchang Gully

龙昌峡

　　龙昌峡长约6公里，原来又叫龙船峡，幽深地峡谷隐天蔽日，龙昌峡均宽不足二十米，两岸似斧劈刀削一般，笔直的冲上蓝天。悬崖上的岩棺赫然可见。唐代著名诗人杜甫曾游览此峡，留有诗篇《西壤溪》，诗中是这样描述龙昌峡的：

迢迢水出走长蛇

怀抱江村在野牙

一叶兰舟龙洞府

数间茅屋野人家

　　从诗人的笔中你能感受大诗人对龙昌峡自然景观的真实描述和赞美，同时也展现了当时生活在神农溪上的人们凄苦的生活状态。诗中所写的"龙洞府"就是今天的龙昌峡，《舆地纪胜》亦有"此洞非石洞，乃山水之奇观也，一洞十里、可浮舟往来"的记载。

Longchang Gully, 6km long, is the former Dragon Boat Gully, a tranquil and pleasantly cool place. On average Longchang Gully is less than 20m wide, the banks are dangerous cliffs reaching sky. In the steep you will see coffins, a wonder of the world. Du Fu, the great poet of Tang Dynasty ever came here, this trip was proved by his great poem Xi Rang Xi:

The river runs like a snake

Village in her arms,

A boat flies over Long Dong Fu (Dragon's Cave)

A few cottages passed by in a moment

岩棺　　Coffins in the crevices

The poem describes scenic views of Longchang Gully and sings high great nature, also presents the hard life of Shen Nong Xi people. Long Dong Fu as mentioned in the poem is today's Longchang Gully according to Wonders of Yudi (Yu Di Ji Sheng), the cave is not stone, but a wonder of nature, a cave lasts 10km, the channel for boats.

　　过了龙昌峡，视觉渐渐地变得开阔起来。这时你也会从一路梦幻般的旅程遐想中回过神来，心中会默默无语的感叹神农溪之美！纤夫之美！

　　西壤口将是你神农溪漂流的终点，古时的西壤口曾是一个刀光剑影的古战场，农民起义军屯兵十万的住地，三国时期刘备烧船断道阻陆逊的所在地。这一切，都恍如昨天。

　　神农溪……

Going out Longchang Gully, the views become wider and wider. The moment you may wake up from a tour of dream, and can't suppress your surprise any more, what an amazing Shen Nong Xi!

Xi Rang Kou is the end of Shen Nong Xi drifting. In the history, Xi Rang Kou was ever a battle field stationed by peasants' revolutionary army. Also in Xi Rang Kou, Liu Bei, an emperor of Three-country Dynasty, burned the boats and cut off chase of Lu Xun, marshal of kingdom Wu. The wars of cavalry and thorn seemingly happened hours ago.

Shen Nong Xi...

神农溪上的纤夫

TRACKERS OF SHEN NONG XI

　　他们是太阳的骄子。

　　早上，太阳涨红脸忍受着分娩的阵痛挪进神农溪口子，他们便拉着生命之舟赤条条地从太阳盆腔里走了出来。

　　"吆哦吆哦！"

　　"嘿呵！"

　　古老原始的神农溪纤夫号子，贴着石壁贴着溪流贴着卵石滩，在窄窄的峡谷里荡来漾去，漾去荡来。

　　溪边妹子不抬头地洗着衣裳，两只耳朵却远远地放着了望哨。凭着号子声的大小，溪边妹子知道拉纤的纤夫离自己还有多远，而且能从纷杂的号子声中一下辨认出相好的那个"他"来。一丝不挂的纤夫，在溪边妹子眼里算不得一回事。

　　是的呗，穿着裤子在水里趟，湿裤子裹身会把皮肉磨烂的。都是父母所生，什么稀奇？赤条条就赤条条，神农溪上的纤夫祖祖辈辈都是这么驾船的。

　　世上的好些事啊，都是叫人说得神乎其神了的。

　　纤夫们嚓嚓踩着鹅卵石来到溪边妹子跟前，溪边妹子眼睛盯着溪水只顾搓洗衣裳，不予理睬。相好的那个"他"擦身过，悄悄地将城里买的"东西"丢在洗衣石边，不吭声地走了；有心计的溪边妹子早有准备，赶紧拿件衣裳把"东西"盖住。哎，事情做得尽管巧妙，还是让人看见了。一阵哈哈爆响，清清的溪水里映出张张笑脸，笑得像那艳艳的山茶花。

　　是该死的神农溪泄了密！

　　溪边妹子捡个鹅卵石使劲地扔进溪流里，水花溅起，惹得人们和溪水一起大笑起来。

神农溪上拉纤曲 Boatmen track the boat with work song in Shennong Stream

They are sons of the sun.

In the morning, the blushing sun, like a childbearing women, shamble toward Shen Nong Xi, the men, tracking a boat of life, go out of the pelvis of sun.

"Yo······"

"Ho······"

It's an old song of Tracker popular in Shen Nong Xi, stepping on stone, spring and screes, the trackers are measuring the gully again and again using their feet.

At riverside, a girl is washing clothes, she guesses the distance from the trackers according to the sound of the song, She is able to identify which is sung by their love. In her eyes, tracker's naked body is not a shame.

About this issue, the girl has her own opinions, the men work in water all day, if body is wrapped by wet clothes, the skin may be injured. Since everybody is born in nature, nothing need be hidden. Trackers of Shen Nong Xi, since their ancestors, has been bare facing Shen Nong Xi in everyday.

激流滩头船受了阻。

成前倾姿式拉纤的纤夫五体投地，屁股朝天，手脚并用地在卵石滩上爬行；力的较量，斗志的较量，一双双眼珠子鼓得要弹出来。脸上的汗珠子一粒一粒滚动着，抖落到卵石上，立即碎成一朵朵崖腊梅。

肩上的份量突然减轻了。吭哧吭哧的纤夫一抹脸上的汗珠子，憨憨的笑了。身后来了添的。添滩的妹子姿势正好与纤夫们相反。双手攥住纤绳，仰面朝天呈倒拔杨柳状，脚蹬得鹅卵石哗哗响，脸蛋子撑得蜜桔一样红。纤夫们来了蛮劲，号子喊得震天响，直把个船头扯得翘上了天。

拉上一滩又一滩。

走过一湾又一湾。

崖畔上的纤槽越勒越深，石壁上的篙坑越捣越大。古往今来，朝朝暮暮，年年岁岁，一代代神农溪纤夫用纤绳和篙子记录着水上春秋，不曾有过丝毫疏忽。

在神农峡中体验纤夫拉纤的全过程　Tracker's Journey through Shennong Gul

There are a lot of interesting stories about Shen Nong Xi.

Tracker has passed by the girl at riverside, you may say nothing happened, really? Look at the water, you will see the girl is covering something in the river with the clothes, what's it? A present that a tracker bought the girl. Nobody, but Shen Nong Xi witnessed what happened, when the present falls in the water, a sound is heard by everybody, haw-haw laughs fly over the river, the water mirror their smile.

It is Shen Nong Xi that disclosed this secret!
The girl will throw a stone at the men, water splashes, spectators and the brook, all are laughing.

Sometimes, the boat may fall in riptides or shoals.

The Tracker will pull the rope with full force, head nearly touches the ground, creeping on the screes. This is a competition of force and will, trackers open wide their eyes, sweat rains to the screes, leaving a picture of plums on the stones.

But soon the riptides or shoals are defeated, the load on shoulder is released, they will wipe off the sweat on the face, simpering at each other. Sometimes girls may help them, face blushes like an orange. Standing before girls, men feel unprecedented power in their body, boat flies over one place after another, like a happy bird.

船终于拉到了卸货点叶子坝。

这是大山深处的一个小镇。依山傍水的穿架子木屋把小镇装扮得典雅古朴，风姿秀逸。船要在这里卸货装货。卸货装货是搬运工的事，用不着纤夫们操心。酒店里的吃喝声大于滩上的号子声。

痛痛快快地吃痛痛快快地喝痛痛快快地说痛痛快快地笑……一切的一切只图个痛痛快快。狂放不羁的神农溪造就了纤夫们狂放不羁的性格。野里日气的玩笑开得炒菜的大嫂哭笑不得，伸过来的锅铲子若是躲闪不及，正好磕在头上。哈哈声中纤夫们添了酒兴添了食欲，大喊大叫上酒上菜，姑爷今天不喝成个酒神仙决不上船。大碗大碗的苞谷酒，烧得纤夫们脸红脖子红眼珠子红。说话喷出的酒气，直冲得端盘子的妹子车轱辘似地调过头去。

吃饱了喝足了乐够了纤夫们歪歪倒倒回了船。

吃得喝得做得睡得才算是神农溪上的纤夫。刚才还海吹神讪快活得忘了天地日月的纤夫，钻进船舱便鼾声如雷，头枕着溪流呼噜呼噜进入了梦乡。

下力人最是体贴下力人。瞌睡睡不好哪有劲放滩？下水比上水更操心啦！搬运工起肩装舱轻起轻落，生怕惊跑了纤夫们的好梦。

"开船喽！"

艄工一声喊，纤夫们一个个揉着惺忪的眼睛钻出船舱，一个懒腰一伸，三五两下脱光衣裳，各就各位。

涉水而行
A Trip on Water

Year by year, generation by generation, deep towline slot is left in the cliffs, pole dent left in the stone, rope and pole wrote their life. The boat reached Dian Zi Ba, a discharge dock.

It is a town hidden in mountains. Wooden house is the old and mystery dress of the town, makes it graceful and elegant. Boats of Shen Nong Xi will be loaded or unloaded in this town. Loading or unloading is none of Tracker's business, they will have a big dinner in restaurant.

Drinking, cheers, guess fingers, it's time to indulge the limited leisure, they will never constrain themselves, like Shen Nong Xi, which forges trackers' unruly manners. In the restaurant, they played blue jokes with the hostess, but should beware of the hostess's scoop in hands.

The joke stimulates trackers' appetite, they called waitress to add dishes, bowls of bract wine burns red their face and neck, the fume of wine the spit is so intolerable that the young waitress wouldn't face them.

After dinner, they came back to boat.

叶子坝的轿夫 Sedan Carriers of Yeziba

一天最紧张最劳累的时辰开始了。

窄窄的浅浅的神农溪给纤夫们施展才能的天地太小太小，篙子不用捏上颠头就能点着两岸石壁，负重的船体底板贴紧水下鹅卵石哗哗地行进，听起来犹如陆地行舟。

调头离岸的船，经湍急的溪水轻轻一推，转眼之间变成了一把水上飞梭。

"嗨！"

"呀！"

飞速前进的船只允许纤夫喊号子吐单字。

捉紧艄把子的纤夫眉宇间透出一股虎虎雄风，浑身肌肉金龟似地挤压拱动，直扳得艄颠子如同乌龙摆尾，在溪流里搅起团团雪花浪。

似云中出，如雾中来，崖墩墩上的船棺也开始放滩……那是祖先留下的。当年，祖先也像他们一样在这条溪上摸爬滚打，拉纤放滩。

崖上的飞梭水上的飞梭同时在穿梭。

激流引爆了纤夫们的强烈征服欲。

滩上窜起小山样的劈头浪，恶魔般要吞食射来的飞梭。迎着浪头去哟，穿着浪头过哟！蓦地，人船射进了浪里；转眼，又从浪里射了出来。纤夫们赤条条的身子几经溪水打磨，跟擦亮了的巴氏铜剑样光闪闪，与高高悬在空中的太阳展开了光的对射，不时爆出一个个耀眼的光点。形同水鬼样的礁石出现了。

放滩 Sail Shoal

42

In no minutes, in thunder-like snore, trackers fall in sweet dreams, Shen Nong Xi is their pillow.

The poor sympathize the poor. The moment, hamals are unloading the boat, they lift their steps as gentle as possible, afraid to awake trackers' sweet dreams.

" Weigh anchor!"

Tracker immediately get up, put off clothes, stand their posts in a few minutes.

Another hard day starts.

The narrow, shallow Sheng Nong Xi make Tracker easy to drive, pole reaches the cliffs on both banks, the boat bottom strikes the cobbles in the water, it sounds that the boat is running on land.

The boat may speed up like a shuttle with help of torrent.

"Hai!"

"Wow!"

They have no time to spit more words to express their surprise.

板着一副狰狞面孔的礁石，渴望射来的船头碰撞。一次次碰碎船头，一次次葬身鱼腹。纤夫们用血和肉换来了闯礁二十字诀："对着礁石去，大吉又大利；躲着礁石走，大祸要临头。"天神爷，呈现在眼前的场面是何等惊险何等壮观！船头不偏不倚不躲不闪，一条线地对着礁石射去，那架势简直像是要去跟礁石拼命，非把礁石钻它个窟窿不行；就在船头要碰上礁石的一刹那，纤夫们大喝一声抢扳艄头，只见船头一扭，船轻轻松松贴着礁石过去了。接着，又射向了另一个礁石。

放过一滩又一滩。

闯过一礁又一礁。

斗红了眼的纤夫，只恨险滩太少，恶礁太少，积蓄在体内的能量没法释放完。于是在心底对神农溪发出声声祈求：神农溪啊，神农溪，你再现几道险滩吧，你再现几个恶礁吧！回答纤夫们的是溪水败北的喘息声。

"哦嗬嗬嗬！"

船慢慢减速驶向与长江交汇处神农溪口，夕阳朝归来的娇子投来热烘烘的吻，亲热不够，疼爱不够。

绵竹峡中的炊烟 Home in Mianzhu Gully

44

They hold rudder firmly, muscle tensioned, looking like turtle shell. The rudder acts like tail of dragon, dancing in spoondrift.

The moment you will see the heritage of ancestors, the coffin on the cliff. They men in the coffin were also trackers of Shen Nong Xi.

Hilly tides fly on the shoal, the shuttle hit the billow, punch the billow, suddenly, the boat is swallowed, but soon thrown by billows. Polished by the stormy water, Tracker's skin looks glittery like a copper thorn, echoing with the brilliant sun.

Ferocious reefs are wait to capture a boat, sometimes they tear off boat head, sometimes they pull Tracker into fish's mouth, Tracker sum up a 20-word recipe: "beat the reef, survival is ahead, escape the reef, catastrophe befall". It's a journey to hell, the boat will exactly hit the reef, regardless of their life, seemingly no choice but drill through the reef; however, when the boat head is nearly touching the boat head, the boat immediately zigs, in one second, it has escaped from the reef, and shoot at another reef.

Cross one shoal after another!

Cross one reef after another!

Trackers are frenzied bulls, they wish to challenge more dangerous shoals and reefs, they have too many energy to release. They even beg the God, "encore, shoals and reefs", but only their breath echoes in the sky.

"O...he..."

Boat runs slowly toward Shen Nong Xi, the joint to Chang Jiang River, where the sun is waiting for its sons, triumphal warriors.

纤夫石

STONE OF TRACKER

直立江边，默默含情。

腰间，叫纤绳勒出了一圈一圈的沟槽，细了许多，身段儿看上去则显得更加苗条，楚楚动人。

它们是纤夫的相好，因而叫"纤夫石"。

纤夫拉纤拉累了，纤夫石是歇气的墩。纤夫将纤绳往它们腰间一拴，歇过气后再上路；激浪滩头，船顶牛要退回去，纤夫石是拴牛的桩。纤夫把纤绳往它们身上一套，野牛样的船便服服贴贴地被牵了回来；夜幕降临，船靠岸歇息，纤夫石是纤夫绾梦的"梦花树"。劳累了一天的纤夫啊，将船牢牢地拴在它们身上，头枕着峡江，进入了甜甜的梦乡，所做的梦啊，尽数绾在了这些"梦花树"上。

三峡纤夫石，是"情石"。

在纤夫眼里，那纤夫石就是自己的女人。你看她直直地立在江边，眉头紧锁，神情专注地望着峡口子归来的帆船，眼睛一眨不眨；女人命苦。嫁给了纤夫，就等于变成了一头牛，家里一应大小事都搁在了她肩上。种田、喂猪、生儿育女，一天从早忙到晚，难得有个歇气的时候。女人啦，是活生生的纤夫石。她那腰间一圈一圈的纤痕，是生活的纤绳生生给勒出来的。

STONE OF TRACKER

Standing at riverside, full of love in eyes.

Towline print was left on the stone, they look slimmer and more graceful.

They are loves of trackers, they are called Stone of Tracker.

The Stone is trackers' dak. Trackers tie the towline to the stone, sit down and take a break; in shoals, when the boat runs aground, the stone will be lifesaver of trackers, anchored to the stone, the boat will obediently go back to calm; at night, when the boat parks, the Stone is a Tree of Dream, trackers will fasten the towline to the stone, relieve day's fatigue. They pillow on screes, captured by a sweet dream soon, all their dreams are coiled around the Tree of Dream.

Stone of Tracker, the love of Trackers.

In some sense, the Stone is love of Trackers. She stands at river, eyes on the gem of sky, seemingly wait for trackers on the way back like a wife. Trackers wives leads a hard life, they work hard all day, farming, breeding, giving birth and looking after kids. The Stone act like the trackers wives. The Wife has engraved wrinkles on her body.

Women can endure hardship, but can't enjoy the hardship.

巫峡岸边的纤痕 Towline Slot of Wu Strait

48

Men are their loyal listeners, every time men go home, at table women start wagging their tongue, saying that it was the biggest mistake to marry trackers.

They said, they didn't enjoy life a little, had no fun all life. Whatever women say, smile still hang in men's face, as if an interesting story is told. That's true, women supports the home, all housework are shouldered by women, they need an exit to release the mood piled up in their heart, as they wish to untie the towline after work. Trackers think their wives are the best women in the world, only their wives care for them best.

Men care for women too. At bed, they put hands on women's forehead, counting the wrinkles engraved by busy housework, worries, miss, like the print left on the Stone by towline. They wish to use their hands to cure women's wrinkles, as they know, they two are the passengers in the same boat, they need join hands to sail cross the billows all the way.

In women's imagination, the Stone of Tracker is like their illfated husband. They often say, man is an ox, the towline on his shoulder is the yoke, boat is the plough, tracking is plowing. Every day, men work on water, wearing sun and moon, only the river hears their heavy breath, they track the boat, as they track their fate. In Summer, sun burns like fire; while in Winter, bise punches like knife, nothing is harder than tracking, nobody is more pitiful is than their husbands.

可怜的女人哦，吃得苦，肚子里却装不得苦。

男人一趟生意走完回到家里，女人把饭菜做好一端上桌子，便开始数数拉拉地诉苦：说这辈子没长后眼睛，千不该万不该嫁给纤夫。

一天吃没吃个好，穿没穿个好，日子过得比黄连还要苦。男人笑眯眯地听着，一概不生气。只顾喝酒，只顾吃菜，就当是女人在拉家常。生个什么气呢？女人说的没有假，句句是实话。人心都是肉长的。你成天在外面东跑西跑，她在家里一年苦上头，在你面前诉诉苦是什么大不了的事！诉诉诉，有苦只管诉。在纤夫看来，女人诉苦就好比拉纤拉累了卸肩上的纤绳，卸掉了，身上也就轻松了。女人是世上最好的女人。最是懂得心疼男人。别看女人恶声恼气地嘴巴打死人，心疼男人可心疼在实处。看见不？诉说不上几句，她又忙着给男人碗里拈菜，生怕男人没吃得。

女人心疼男人，男人自然就心疼女人。睡在被窝里，纤夫总爱摸女人的额头。轻轻的，慢慢的，一下一下地摸。苦命的女人，拉扯家口，操心劳碌，皱纹过早地爬上了额头。那一条条皱纹，也是生活的纤绳生生给勒出来的呀！纤夫心里酸酸的，颤颤的，一下一下地摸着女人的额头，像是要把心里所有的疼爱抹上女人的额头，将那一条条皱纹填平。两人立的家，谁说只有女人苦呢？男人也苦。

在女人眼里，那纤夫石活灵活现就是自己那苦命的男人。男人也是头牛。你看那勒在肩上的纤绳，跟架在牛背上的轭头有什么两样？四肢着地拉纤，跟牛犁田又有什么两样？男人是一头牛，船是一张犁。一年四季，一根纤绳勒在肩上，吭哧吭哧地在江上犁得直喘粗气。拉纤的日子，那不叫日子！叫磨命。盛夏，身上叫毒日头烙得焦煳，跟蛇样一层层蜕皮；隆冬，脚手一行比得上拉纤苦？没有。叫凛冽的寒风吹得皲裂出一条条鱼腮样的口子，生血直冒。世上千般苦，还有哪 三峡里拉纤还不光是苦哦，还有险。凶滩恶水，纤夫吃的是阎王爷门前的一碗饭，弄不好就会叫纤绳拖下水，赤条条的死在江里。苦命的男人，不像女人肚子里装不住苦。男人嘴巴紧得像上了锁，纵有千般苦楚，他也不会向你吐露一星半点。男人是头牛，是头闷性子牛，是头棒棒打鞭子抽哼都不哼一声的闷性子牛！女人心疼自己的男人就心疼在这一点上。男人上船走生意一出峡，就在屋里扳起指头子算，扒起眼皮子望。那峡里的纤夫石哦，还真是望成了人！一到夜里，纤夫石就变成男人走进了梦中，两个亲亲热热地搂在一起，说也有了，笑也有了。于是，三峡里就有了望郎石；于是，三峡里就有了望郎峰；于是……伴随着望郎石和望郎峰的相思故事啊，就像那峡里春江水生泡子，一个接一个地冒了出来。

However, women's bigger worry is men's risk posed by the dangerous river. Every trip is a survival from hell. Nevertheless, whatever happened, men will never disclose their psyche, they prefer bearing everything alone. Man is like a dumb ox, any whip can't make it open mouth. Women's care is drawn by men's such a temper. From the moment man goes out, the wife starts to count his day back, like the stone watching on riverbank.

At night, the Stone is the men in bed, she made love, chat, have fun with him in the dream. This is told by the stories about Waiting Stone, Waiting Cliff still standing at riverbank

Woman is housewife, man is source of economy.

The family lives on the towline on men's shoulder, which has engraved deep scar lines on trackers' skin. At night, women kiss these scars, tears down to her eyes. What a true love it is!

Stone of Tracker, the men in women's eyes, the women in men's eyes, anchor men and women's home. Men and women, hold the towline of life, shoulder on shoulder, sing the song of boatmen, fight against shoals and reefs. Their sweat beans echoes with brilliant sunlight.

Trackers lead a hard life, but like the bitter buckwheat growing on the cliff, they also have sweet time. They live in true love, mutual care, they live a happy life.

徐光宣　农耕（朱砂土）

Stone of Tracker belongs to men, also belongs to women, it records love of men and women. The longer the print of towline extends, the longer their love is, the deeper the towline slot grows, the deeper their love is.

【NOTES】
Stone of Tracker: a stake made of stone, planted at riverside, used to anchor trackers. There are countless such stones in Three-strait, many of them have been engraved deep slot by the towline.
Tree of Dream: a soft bush, called Tree of Dream by villagers of Tujia Nationality. Every time the people made a good dream, they will coil the tree a circle with vine, wishing to retain the good dream.

Towline Slot
Boat trackers, should the towline, sing the songs of boatmen, measure the shoals and reefs of Three-strait again and again with their feet, 3, 4-inch-deep slots are left on the stone, witness their hard life.

Pole Dent
Three-strait is famous for narrow runway, big fall, riptides, dangerous shoals, boat is the traffic tool of ancient people through the strait, pole is boatmen's weapon to fight against billows, today, deeper pole dents were left on the stone, recorded trackers' bloody battle against the river.

女人操持家务，还得男人弄回来哩！

男人是家里顶梁柱。家里的一切开销，得靠男人肩上那根纤绳拉回来。为了拉扯这个家，男人肩膀上的茧子，叫纤绳勒掉一层又一层，跟那纤夫石一样，勒出了一条深深的茧槽。女人夜里躺在男人怀里，总爱摸男人的肩膀。那深深的茧槽，最是动情处，摸着摸着，禁不住泪珠子一颗一颗地滚了出来。

三峡纤夫石，在男人眼里是女人；在女人眼里是男人，拴着"家"这条船。生活的纤绳啦，勒在男人肩上，勒在女人肩上，男人女人在同一条纤道上攀爬，于深沉的号子声中，汗淋淋地将"家"这条船拉上一滩又一滩。

别看纤夫家里日子，说来说去总说不掉一个"苦"字。那苦还真像峡里崖墩墩上种的苦荞，苦中有甜哩！夫妻之间你心疼我，我心疼你，小日子掺和着几分真情，过得也舒心，也如意。比起那些虚情假意、同床异梦的凑合夫妻，要美气得多！

三峡的纤夫石属于男人，属于女人，男人女人的恩恩爱爱全刻在上面。那纤痕有多长，纤夫跟女人的情便有多长；那纤痕有多深，纤夫跟女人的爱便有多深。

徐光宣　日本游客与朱砂土村民交流

54

巴东民间舞蹈"撒尔嗬"

　　巴东"撒尔嗬"又称"打丧鼓",是土家族先民在长期的生产与生活中所形成的独特习俗。史称:"巴人尚武,父母死丧,鼓以道哀,其众必跳,其跳必狂"。"击鼓踏歌以兴哀"。用亦歌亦舞的方式悼念死者,世代承袭,至今保持着浓厚的巴人遗风。古代巴人的祭祀舞蹈,在大量吸收了楚、汉民间舞蹈的同时,在形式和内容上不但形成了土家人的文化,使它地方化、民族化。跳"撒尔嗬"既是一种民俗,同时也表达了巴人特有的生死观。人死只不过是灵魂离开躯体,在另一层意义上它又是再生。因此跳"撒尔嗬"哀而不悲,而是以欢快的歌舞来表现。

巴东古民居　Old Architecture of Badong

BADONG'S DANCING SA ER HE

Sa Er He, also known as "Funeral Drum", is a distinct custom of Tujia Nationality with a history of thousands of years. According to historical records, "Ba people like Wushu, they strike drum at funeral of parents to express mourning, and all attendants dance crazily". The grieve over the death through singing and dancing. Today, as a custom of Ba people, this dance passes down the lifestyle of old ages. The fete dance of ancient Ba people borrowed the popular dance of states Chu and Han, and formed Tujia Nationality's own culture both in form and content, recognized as the nation's valuable heritage. Sa Er Ge dance is not only a folk, but also expresses Ba People's values on death. In their mind, the death is just a departure of soul from body, and a rebirth of soul. So Sa Er He dance is grieving but not mournful, it expressed the people's sentiment in lively rhythm.

民间舞蹈 "牛擦痒" Folk Dance: Rutting Bull

民间舞蹈 "燕儿含泥" Folk Dance: Swift Carries Earth

清. 同治版《巴东县志》上记载："旧俗殁之日，其家置酒席，邀亲友，鸣金伐鼓，歌舞达旦，或一夕，或三五夕"。

跳"撒尔嗬"主要流行于神农溪流域和清江流域的野三关、清太坪、白沙坪、长岭、泗淌、杨柳池、马家一带。俗有"听到丧鼓响，脚板儿就发痒"之说。在这些土家族聚居的地方，每逢有人过世，乡邻闻讯从四面八方翻山越岭赶来悼念逝者。当晚在灵柩前放置一牛皮大鼓，由一掌鼓的歌师击鼓喊歌，二人踏着鼓点相对而舞（或四人对跳称"穿花"）并和歌。边舞边唱，有时不等舞毕，他人争着上场替换。其锣鼓紧凑，歌声高昂豪放，舞姿粗犷古朴，动作多为模仿山中飞禽走兽和一些农事动作。表演通宵达旦。歌唱的内容有颂古人、颂亡人、唱地名、解歌、怀胎歌及爱情故事等等。常用的曲调有：1.《叫歌》（又叫"待师"），2.《摇丧》，3.《吆女儿合》，4.《哑谜子合》，5.《怀胎歌》，6.《燕儿衔泥》（又叫"耍五巾"），7.《长声哨》，8.《吆姑姐筛锣》，9.《螃蟹歌》等。

土家族的丧礼 Funeral of Tujia Nationality

According to "*Log of Badong County*" made in Tongzhi period of Qing Dynasty: at funerals, relatives and friends are invited to feast, they strike drum, singing and dancing, overnight, or for 3 to 5 days.

Sa Er He is popular in Yeshanguan, Qingtaiping, Baishaping, Changling, Sitang, Yangliuchi, Majia in Shennongxi and Qingjiang catchment, this is proved by a jingle "funeral bell rings, dance and sing". In villages of Tujia Nationality, when a funeral is held, the people from near or faraway, across the mountains or rivers gather at a big drum made of ox skin, one man strike the drum while singing, two men dance (or four men dance, called "Chuan Hua"), facing to each other. Other people will substitute them in turn. The drum strike fast, song shocks ears, gesture is simple and wild, some imitate the beast, some imitate farming activities. The performance will be on show overnight, the song sings high ancestors, , the dead, toponym, birth, love, etc. The reserved songs include: 1. Song of Shouting ("Dai Shi"); 2. Rock the Death; 3. Yao Nu Er He; 4. Ya Mi Zi He, 5. Birth Song; 6. Swift Carries Earth (Shua Wu Jin); 7. Chang Sheng Shao; 8. Sister Sings Gong; 9. Song of Grabs.

古代巴人的跳"撒尔嗬"，是为了悼念亡者，更是为了繁育后代。"撒尔嗬"舞中很明显地表现出古代巴人对生殖的需求和崇尚，舞蹈中的"牛擦痒"、"猛虎下山"、"犀牛望月"、"凤凰闪翅"、"虎抱头"、"双狮抢球"等舞蹈动作，喻意着男人们渴望从它们身上获取力量和旺盛的生命力，来繁衍后代，使巴人部落人丁兴旺。在"撒尔嗬"中还有表现异性交媾动作的"狗连裆"，由此看来古代巴人通过"淫祀"的场合，来进行性教育，也反映出古代巴人的"性"崇拜和对猛虎、犀牛、雄狮的骠悍、雄健之美的崇尚！

"撒尔嗬"是土家人一种男性双人对跳的舞蹈，对数不受限制，如果四个人一起跳，则以双人舞为组合，四个舞者按逆时针方向依次对跳，穿插交换位置；若众人一起合舞，则围成圆圈，沿逆时针方向舞动，而不需再互相换位或穿插。据土家人的传说，土家人的跳"撒尔嗬"，是庄子"鼓盆歌"的沿袭。

古宅童趣 Childhood in Old House

民间舞蹈"撒尔嗬"，是土家民族文化一绝。国际友人在观看"撒尔嗬"后，将其称之为"东方迪斯科"。

Sa Er He is not only to mourn the dead, but also sing for the born. Sa Er Ha also expresses Ba people's worship toward sex and birth, a lot of actions in the dance such as Rutting Bull, Tiger down Mountain, Rhinoceros Looks Up Moon, Phoenix Wings, Tiger Holds Head, Two Lions Fight for Ball, express men's desire for force and power of life, and wishes to give birth. They even show the actions of animal's sex, this is called "sex sacrifice", and wish to widespread sex education. The dance also reflects the ancient Ba people's worship toward sex and bravery, mightiness of beasts such as tiger, rhinoceros and lions.

土家族的老寿星 Longevity Star of Tujia Nationality

民间舞蹈 "牛擦痒" Folk Dance: Rutting Bull

Sa Er He is a Double Men dance, pairs of men dance toward each other. If four men take part in, they will be divided in pairs, and move anti-clockwise, exchange positions in turn; if more people join the dance, they will stand in a circle, and move anti-clockwise, no need exchange positions or cross each other. According to legends of Tujia Nationality, Sa Er He comes from "Drum Basin Song" of Zhuangzi, a great ancient ideologist.

Sa Er He is a characteristic civilian dance, a valuable heritage of the nation, it is called "Eastern Disco" by foreign audience.

原始生产工具石磨作坊 Millstone Workshop

独放异彩的巴东堂戏
DISTINCT BADONG TANG OPERA

堂戏也称花鼓戏，俗称踩堂戏、稿荐戏、人大戏。堂戏是以巴东方言入曲和道白；用"大筒子腔"（梁山调）、"小筒子腔"（南、北路）和其他曲牌、小调演唱；伴以管、弦、打击乐器及人声帮和；由艺人化妆登台按一定程式当众表演现实生活、历史故事和神话传说等题材的地方戏。

Badong Tang Opera, also known as Caitang Opera, Gaojian Opera, Renda Opera. It employs accent of Badong as music and dialogue; it borrows the descant of "Da Liang Zi" (Liang Shan melody), "Xiao Tong Zi" (south school, north school) and other intonations and tune; its musical instrument includes organs, chords, percussion instrument, as well as human voices; they perform local operas on the stage and have a full set of rules, the script is taken from daily life, historical stories, myth, legends, etc.

Badong Tang Opera comes from the popular "Huagu Dance" for purpose of blessings and celebrating, it is still on show in Shen Nong Xi Stream in north side of Changjiang River, Badong County, En'shi Autonomous Prefecture, Hubei, it is at the age over 300 years.

Badong Tang Opera is born in civilian art of Badong, it is easy to understand, telling the stories occurring in our daily life. It artfully reflects the people's sentiment. It is called Five Golden Flowers of culture and art of En'shi Prefecture together with South Opera, Nuo Opera, Deng Opera, Liuzi Opera, with distinct charm among nationwide 380 opera types.

在巴东乡间深受群众喜爱的巴东堂戏　　Badong Tang Opera

　　堂戏起源于民间还愿酬神和喜庆贺喜的"跳'花鼓子'"，至今流行在湖北省恩施自治州巴东县长江北岸的神农溪流域，有"堂戏三百年"之说

　　堂戏在巴东江北民间文艺的土壤中产生，贴近生活、通俗易懂，艺术地表达了人民群众的喜怒哀乐，深受群众欢迎。因此，堂戏同南剧、傩戏、灯戏、柳子戏一道，被称为恩施州民族地区文化艺术中的"五朵金花"，是全国三百八十多个各具特色的地方戏中独放异彩的剧种。

Badong Tang Opera was formerly called Opera of Tang Dynasty. About this name there is a beautiful story. One time, Li Shimin of the Tang Dynasty promised to save an old dragon violating God's rules, but he failed. Later the dragon implead him in Hell, one day in dream Li Shimin came to hell and was revenged by the dragon, judge Cui saved him and prolonged his life, to show gratitude to gods, Li commanded nationwide people to play Tang Opera, that's why it is also called Opera of Tang Dynasty. Another story is also about this name, still in Tang Dynasty, when Wu Zetian occupied the emperor's chair, the old subjects of Tang Dynasty fought against her, Xue Gang, one of the fighters, was defeated by Wu Sansi, Wu Zetian's general, he fled to the forest of Shennongjia, and married Ji Luanying, a female general. From then on, the couple lived there and in vented an opera, they put on the stage the stories as described in the festival lantern of Chang'an, capital of Tang Dynasty, soon the game was widely spread, the people later called it Opera of Tang Dynasty.

It is also said that, the opera is brought to here by a royal opera player of Emperor Li Longji after "Riot of An & Shi". In addition to Tang Opera, shadow puppet (local people called it "Pi Da Zai") is also popular in north bank of Changjiang in Badong. The music of shadow puppet is

传统歌舞 Folk Dance

　　巴东堂戏，曾被称为"唐戏"。据其流传地区的艺人和民间传说：唐太宗李世民许愿搭救犯了天条的泾河老龙，但最终没能保住老龙的性命。索命的老龙把李世民告到阴司，李世民梦游地府，得崔判官相助反倒添寿还阳，因而酬神还愿唱起了堂戏，遂有唐戏之称。民间还流传说武则天临朝称帝，不服的老臣宿将举兵反抗，"通城虎"薛刚反唐兵败后，被武三思大军追赶，从九焰山经房州（今房县、保康、竹山、竹溪一带）遁入神农架原始森林中，途经紫竹河与落草女将纪鸾英结为夫妻，随后在巴东边界大九湖的"挂字号"筑台扎营、点将练兵。闲暇时为娱乐九营将士，同纪鸾英夫妻二人，仿长安京城花灯上的人物故事分扮角色作戏，从此流传后世，衍为唐戏

徐光宣　朱砂土民俗

66

正在表演巴山舞的土家青年　Young Bashan Dancers on Show

similar to that of Xiao Tong Zi of Tang Opera, so local opera players mostly are shadow puppet singers. In shadow puppet, there is a role called "Zha Wa Zi", also called "Pao Tang Zi" or "Can Jun", "Can Jun" is an opera of Tang Dynasty. Like Tang Opera, shadow puppet is also an art heritage born in Tang Dynasty.

Unlike other operas, Tang Opera didn't sing high the Li Cunxu, emperor Zhuangzong of Later Tang Dynasty (Houtang), it integrated emperors Zhuangzong and Taizong in one character. So there are no historical records proving these legends, so Tang Opera's so long history can't be verified, on the other hand, Tang Opera was formerly played in a big square table in living hall ("Tang" in Pin Yin), and characterized by unique "Tang Bu" (three paces and a half), so in 1956, Ran Ruiquan, an expert of Badong Tang Opera officially named this opera "Badong Tang Opera", briefly referred as Tang Opera.

此外，也有传说堂戏是天宝年间"安史之乱"中，由唐明皇李隆基的梨园弟子流落巴东江北而传入的。巴东江北流行堂戏，也流行皮影戏（当地人叫它"皮打仔"），皮影的声腔与堂戏中的"小筒子"相通，当地的艺人多数既唱皮影戏又唱堂戏。皮影戏中有"喳娃子"这一角色，"喳娃子"又叫"跑堂子"或"参军"，而"参军"正是源于唐代的"参军戏"，可见堂戏同皮影一样，都是唐代古戏……

上述有关的传说中，堂戏没有像有的剧种那样去尊崇后唐庄宗李存勖，或是根本就把唐太宗与后唐庄宗混为了一谈。总之，种种传说都是既无据可考又近于附会，不仅不能证明堂戏有如此久远的历史，也不符合中国戏剧艺术发生和发展的客观实际。其次，由于堂戏最初是在农家堂屋中以大方桌为台演出，又有"左一右二进三退四"这套程式化了的独特的"踩堂步"（俗称"三步半"），因此，巴东堂戏的抢救、挖掘者舟瑞泉等先生们于1956年将这一民族艺术之花正式定名为"巴东踩堂戏"，简称"堂戏"。

In addition to Badong County, Tang Opera also prevails in Jianshi County of En'shi Perfecture, Zigui County and Xingshan County of Yichang City, Shennongjia Forest directly governed by Hubei Province as well as Wushan County of Chongqing. These counties and regions are situated around Three-strait of Changjiang River, except Zigui County where Tang Opera is called "Jiandong Hua Gu Opera", elsewhere the opera is called Tang Opera. What's more, Hefeng County, neighboring south and southeast Badong County, Changyang and Wufeng Tujia Nationality Autonomous Counties of Yichang City also has Tang Opera, but they call it "Yang Hua Liu Opera". According to a survey in 1979, in Baiyiping of Wufeng, five generations are players of Tang Opera, since Zhong Dagu, Tongzhi of Qing Dynasty. According the players of Wufeng, Zigui, Xingshan, Tang Opera came from Badong (Tan Lianjie, Tang Opera, Hubei Volume, China Opera & Music Collection). Badong's Shen Nong Xi, is cradle of Tang Opera.

Tang Opera borrows accent of North Bank of Changjiang River as descant and dialogue, simple in language and beautiful in melody. Its distinct musical instrument includes Si Hu, which has high timbre. Da Tong Zi's long and short music plates have borrowed the songs of trackers of Changjiang River and Shen Nong Xi, melisma employs the back-end players and

神农溪上的歌谣　Songs of Shen Nong Xi

土家族婚俗　Wedding of Tujia Nationality

　　堂戏的流传区域，除开巴东外，还有恩施自治州的建始县、宜昌市的秭归县、兴山县，湖北省直管的神农架林区，以及与巴东接壤的重庆直辖市的巫山县等县、区。这些县、区是连片的山区，都在长江三峡地带。除秭归把堂戏叫"建东花鼓戏"以外，其余地区都叫堂戏。此外，与巴东南部、东南部连界的鹤峰县、宜昌市的长阳、五峰两个土家族自治县，也有巴东传去已经改叫为"杨花柳"了的堂戏。"据1979年调查，堂戏在五峰白溢坪一带，就已经有可考姓名的五代艺人，其最早者为清同治年间钟大古。据五峰、秭归、兴山各地艺人口述，他们县的堂戏早先都是从巴东传去的"（谭联杰：《中国戏曲音乐集·湖北卷·堂戏》稿）。而堂戏的摇篮，则是长江北岸的巴东神农溪流域。

　　堂戏用巴东江北方言入曲和道白，语言朴实，唱腔优美。特色乐器为琵琶头的四胡，音色浓而壮。大筒子腔中的长梢板和短梢板中据说融入有长江及神农溪的船工号子，拖腔时台后艺人同台前观众齐用翻高八度的人声帮和，再加以锣鼓烘托，作为板口结构中的起、落乐句，高亢而又热烈，的确是这一地方戏推进剧情、渲染气氛既独特又积极的艺术手段。

数百年来，巴东堂戏风韵依然。其优秀传统戏有《王麻子打妆》、《山伯访友》、《劝夫》，共有三百多个剧目，巴东溪丘湾、平阳坝、沿渡河各乡镇都有演出队。堂戏是在巴东民间歌舞的土壤程式，经过几百年的演变而渐成体系的。

巫峡帆影 Sail Wu Strait

堂戏艺人长年累月在外出巫山、兴山、秭归、神农架、房县、远安等地演出和观摩外地戏剧表演中，对梁山调、湖北越调、唢呐腔、川剧高腔等凡能接触到的艺术精华大胆借鉴和学习，把各声腔系统中有利于自身发展的剧目、曲调、身段、服饰、中，尤其是在薅草锣鼓的基础上，以"花鼓子"的原生形态，按江北民众的审美观念和欣赏习惯，不断吸收融合梁山调、太平调、汉调、川剧等地方戏曲的腔调、曲牌、场面和表演化妆、场面拿来"为我所用"，结合神农溪当地的声调、语言、风俗和欣赏习惯加以去粗取精、以丰富堂戏的内涵；另一方面，外地艺人进入神农溪流域演出或定居收徒传艺，或与巴东堂戏艺人合班献秘，则直接丰富了堂戏的声腔。

audience's harmonics of raised 8 keys plus drums and gongs. Tang Opera is sonorous and jazzy, it is the ideal and unique way to create atmosphere and attract audience. Badong Tang Opera still survived after hundreds of years. It has over 300 preserved programs including Wangmazi Makes Up, Shanbo Visits Friends, Persuade Husband. It has troupes in many towns such as Xiqiuwan, Pingyangba, Yanduhe. Tang Opera is a great opera system with hundreds of years' history, grown up in the earth of Badong civilian dance and folk songs.

Tang Opera also boldly borrows essence of other operas such as Liangshan Opera, Hubei Yue Opera, Suona, Chuan Opera prevailing in Wu Shan, Xingshan, Zigui, Shennongjia, Fangxian, Yuan'an, etc., including a list of plays, tunes, posture, dressing. According to preferences of North Bank of Changjiang River's audience, it borrowed the intonation, music, scenarios, performance, dressings of Liangshan Opera, Taiping Opera, Han Opera, Chuan Opera to original "Hua Gu Opera", significantly broadened the forms and content of Tang Opera; moreover, the players from elsewhere held shows or taught prentices, or exchanged skills with players of Tang Opera, widely enriched the intonation of Tang Opera.

三峡船夫 BOATMEN OF THREE STRAIT

Three Strait is throat of Changjiang River, and narrow wa
out of boatmen. The boat carries clients' goods, as well a
their negligible life, they measure the narrow channel agai
and again with their feet, brass songs echoing in the valle
till the last drop of candle.

Boatmen of Three Strait, are ascetic monks watching on th
river.

But they are poorer than monks.

像夹墙一样的三峡，对他们来说是一条窄窄的人生通道。他们驾着生命之舟，喊着低沉的号子，年复一年地穿行在这条窄窄的通道里，直到人生终点。

生活苦哦，吃饭一天吃三豆：早晨起来吃黄豆磨的合渣菜豆腐，中午吃绿豆煮的稀饭，晚上吃焖炒的胡豆。你听说过"叮冬菜"么？这可是天下菜谱上找不到的一道名菜。船在峡里遇上了顶头风，就得停靠下来。这叫"扎风"。扎风的时间一长，船上带的菜吃完了，不见人户的峡里无菜可买。这时候，伙夫就上岸捡一瓢指头子大小的卵石子，倒进锅里用油盐酱醋一应佐料炒进味，船夫吃饭时，就以卵石子为菜。用筷子夹一个嘬后往江里一丢，随即传来"叮冬"一声响，"叮冬菜"便由此而得名。

周超　风帆（1985 年）Sail

行船苦哦，闯滩拉纤，他们通常是一丝不挂，赤条条地穿越三峡。死神要他们的命，连声招呼都不打。说死就死了。死在江里的他们，身上不沾一根纱。家里婆娘哭得最叫人伤心落泪的便是那几句千百年流传下来的嚎丧词："你一辈子吃没吃个好，穿没穿个好噢，赤膊来又赤膊去呀，我苦命的人罗！"

生不带来，死不带去。从娘肚子里生出来一个赤条条，死在江里一个赤条条，这便是"赤膊来又赤膊去"。

苦行僧有三峡船夫苦么？没有。苦行僧再吃得差，什么时候吃过"叮冬菜"；苦行僧再穿得破破烂烂，什么时候一丝不挂过？三峡船夫，又是水上的喜乐神。

不。他们比喜乐神还要快活！

说笑起来，没个遮拦，响哈哈打得盖过惊涛骇浪。不说不笑，阎王爷不要。连阎王爷都不要，你还叫什么人么？说哟，笑噢！想怎么说就怎么说，想怎么笑就怎么笑。船一靠码头，他们一个个收拾打扮得像公子少爷，进馆子吃饱了，喝足了，大摇大摆地走进戏院子。演员在台上演戏，他们在台下评戏。公子如何如何，小姐怎样怎样。评到后来便离了谱，满嘴的浑话直往出涌。坐在周围的人听不下去，说你们硬跟放牛场里出来的一样，像些畜牲。他们听了不气不恼。说，算你说对了。我们是"畜牲"。是"官老爷的骡子——快活畜牲。"哈哈声中，越是疯了，越是野了，浑话越是往死里说。

巫峡□ Throat of Wu Strait

　　船上行，赤条条拉纤的他们，会变着戏法儿找江边洗衣裳的女人开玩笑。甚至敢赤条条地一抬腿子从女人们头上跨过去，还说头上不平整。那些洗衣裳的女人也不好惹。婚结了。娃子生了。姑奶奶怕个屁！当船夫们赤条条地从头上跨过去时，顺手扬起棒头倒打上去，准准地打在要害处。直打得他们捂住胯丫子嗷嗷叫喊。如此一来，他们又有话说了："打是疼，骂是爱，不打不骂不挞来。"一阵哈哈爆响，讨来女人们一片刻毒的骂，他们在骂声中高兴得又是蹦，又是跳，像是占了天大个便宜。

　　喜乐神乐，有三峡船夫乐么？喜乐神乐上天，也不会像三峡船夫这么疯，这么野，这么放肆。

Life is poor. Beans are their all day's meals: beancurd plus vegetable pieces are their breakfast, lunch green bean congee, supper is fried broad bean. Have you heard the dish called "Ding Dong", which can't be found in all menu of banquet, but it is boatmen's "Royal Dish". To escape storms, boatmen have to park their boat in somewhere safe, but sometimes vegetables run out but rain still falls, how can they cook? Don't worry, stone is their daintiness, they get some stones from the beach, put in some flavorings and stir-fry them, then a tasteful dish is finished, but they have to spit it out to the river after savoring it, so "Ding Dong" is sound, one disappears, another plays, like beautiful piano music, that's why this dish is called "Ding Dong". Drifting is a trip of venture. Trackers leave no clothes on their body, barebackedly fight against Azrael. They know death may occur at any time, they will not pay anything to hell, except their body. So their woman may repeat a word before the coffin "my illfated, you enjoy nothing all your life, nakedly born, take away nothing from the world."

巫峡晨辉 Good Morning, Wu Strait

巫峡风光　Views of Wu Strait

Nakedly born, take away nothing from the world! This is life of crackers.

Boatmen of Three-strait's life is even poorer than a monk, they don't know what is Ding Dong dish, and they have clothes on body. However, nobody is merrier than Boatmen of Three-strait.

Even the gods!

They laugh louder than backwash. They often said, "Laugh and laugh, or hell will reject you". When boat parks at dock, the boatmen dress themselves like a playboy, go to town, where they will buy an inebriety, afterwards they go to theatre, where play is on show. They flirt with the actress while watching the program, some people may call them "a group of oestrous bulls". "yes", they responded, without angry, continued their fun under the stage.

While on water, they are even bolder.

When seeing women at river, they may play various jokes with them. Some even step over women's faces, and say their face are not smooth. The women are also wild, they are mothers, they don't mind such jokes, some even respond by hitting boatmen's genitals, in such a case, boatmen may say, "hit me, love me", the women then spit out a few dirty words, whatever women say, boatmen always laugh, seemingly they are hearing a song.

巫峡石屏　Stone Screen of Wu Strait

严酷的生活环境，将三峡船夫推到了风口浪尖，他们终日搏击在险相环生的峡江上，需要一种强烈的欢愉情感来替换高度紧张，这样才能求得心理上的平衡。于是，他们就放肆地说；于是，他们就放肆地笑。只有这样，他们才觉得日子过得有滋有味，有斤有两。

　　三峡船夫，性子甚是刚烈。

巫峡帆影　Sail Wu Strait

　　他们骂人骂成了习惯。闯滩搏击风浪，船头船尾骂得一塌糊涂。跟外人如此。跟自家人如此。船一上滩，当驾长的老子不认当引水的儿子；当引水的儿子不认当驾长的老子，是自自然然的事。老子嘴里骂什么，儿子嘴里骂什么，没人觉得奇怪。摇橹的人听见了只当没听见，只顾忙活自己的。别看老子和儿子咬牙切齿骂得火爆爆，那火爆场面会在一瞬间里平息下来。船一下滩，骂声即止。这时，纵有天大的火气也烟消云散了。老子还是老子。儿子还是儿子。走到一起有说有笑，像是什么事也没发生过。哪个要多心怪肠犯嘀咕，一句话就把你给开销了："滩上的话莫拿滩下说！"

官渡风光　Views of Guandu

　　三峡的滩多。滩险。闯滩如同闯鬼门关，是一场生死搏斗，不能有半点马虎。滩上吵架骂人，在某种程度上起到了提醒大家注意力高度集中、齐心协力搏击风浪的作用。这种在常人看来不可思议的事，在三峡里则平平常常，丝毫不值得大惊小怪。"滩上无父子。"古来如此。

　　三峡船夫，有着超人的记忆力。

　　他们驾驶几十吨、乃至上百吨的木船闯荡峡江，风里浪里，所向披靡，那高超的驾驶艺术叫人看了惊叹不已。你要问他们脑壳里装了什么绝技？他们会一笑告诉你："没装什么绝技，只装了一脑壳石头。"这话听起来好玄乎！常常弄得问的人稀泥糊涂不辨东西。其实，不难理解。他们所说的石头，指的就是暗礁。说装了一脑壳石头，就是说装了一脑壳暗礁。三峡从奉节夔门到宜昌南津关，长达两百五十多里，大大小小的礁石数以万计，他们一个个全记在脑壳里。而且能一个个说出名字。什么墩子石怀抱石乌龟石鸭子石蛤蟆石牛鼻子石癞疤子石秤杆子石……一口气百上千来，叫你听得目瞪口呆。

　　三峡的礁石不仅多，而且诡诈。水涨水退，神出鬼没，叫你难以摸清底细。但无论礁石怎样玩鬼，都逃不过三峡船夫那双敏锐的眼睛。就是浑浊的江水把礁石伪装得天衣无缝，不见踪迹，他们也能一眼穿透江水，看个清楚明白，准确地说出礁石的方位。不会错的，"花三埂四泡八尺。"在翻起浪花的下面三尺处有礁石，在凸起水埂的下面四尺处有礁石，江面有沸腾四散的水泡，则水下八尺处有礁石。

Boatmen of Three-strait are happier than the God in heaven.

Living on so inclement conditions, let Boatmen of Three-strait seemingly at mouth of tiger every second, they need a strong joy to release their tension nerves, they say whatever they like, they seek their own joys.

Boatmen of Three-strait are rigid in character.

Swearing is their preferred manner of talking. When storm comes, you may hear abuse full of the boat, even father and son swear at each other. However, when the boat goes back to peace, all abuse immediately disappear, all that they just said flows away with the water, "never mention the quarrelling at shoal", said boatmen.

Actually, swearing is a best way to draw their attention to deal with dangers. As we know, sailing three-strait is a journey to hell, there are countless dangers in the trip, swearing may stimulate everyone's nerves, allow them to keep attentive in the fight against the storms. No one family on boat, that's the boatmen's philosophy.

Boatmen of Three-strait have incredible memory.

They drive tens to hundreds of tons of ship through the Strait, how can they succeed as they roam in the garden? "We have a brain of stones", that's their answer. We need chew this answer. Actually the stone they mentioned is reef, that is to say, they have saved the locations of every reef in their memory, no wonder they can beat all of them so easily. From Kuimen of Fengjie to Nanjinguan of Yichang, there are total 250km, covering thousands of reefs under the water, all of them have been implanted in their brain. They know the name of every reef without a break, e.g. Dun Zi, Huai Bao, Turtle, Duck, Toad, Bull Nose, Scar, Weighbeam...

巫峡风光 Views of Wu Strait

超人的记忆力是拿命换来的。江里那些礁石，都是一个个潜伏在水下的杀手，诡诈且凶残。杀害过他们的祖辈，杀害过他们的父辈。那血淋淋的场面，跟刻刀样刻在了他们脑子里。那是血的记忆。血的记忆，能忘掉么？

峡中飞虹 Rainbow of Wu Strait

窄窄的人生通道，处处是险滩暗礁。三峡船夫，于惊涛骇浪中篙点红日，橹摇明月，出峡进峡只凭一声号子。

三峡船夫，江上的水神！

官渡风光　Views of Guandu

Three-strait hides a lot of reefs, most of them appear and disappear mysteriously, elusory to all reef fighters. However, even the most ghosty reefs will not flee from eyes of boatmen, even though the reef is hidden in the cloudy water, boatmen will tell accurately where the reef lies, they sum up pithy formula, 3 feet below are spoondrifts, 4 feet below are foams, 8 feet below are reefs.

Their memory is saved by the lives of their fathers, their grandfathers, who might have been killed by the fierce reefs hidden in the water. Together with the location of the reefs, the bloody fighting scenes are left in their memory forever.

Narrow waterway of Three-strait, paved by dangerous shoals and ledges, is boatmen's way out. Boatmen of Three-strait, wearing sun and moon, holding poles and paddles, sing high their life through the narrow strait.

Boatmen of Three-strait, god of water!

巴东的摩崖石刻

MOYA STONE CARVINGS

张宏开　石刻（楚蜀鸿沟）

石刻（楚蜀鸿沟）　Stone Carving: Boundary Stone between Chu and Shu

巴东县的摩崖石刻主要集中于长江两岸的岩石峭壁上。自铁棺峡附近的"楚蜀鸿沟"至与秭归交界处红庙岭附近的"化险为夷"，沿江两岸遍布石刻题记（计有摩崖石刻16处，碑刻8块）。

Badong's Moya Stone Carvings mainly occupied the cliffs on both banks of Changjiang River. Especially between the "Boundary Stone between Chu and Shu" (near Strait Tieguan) and "Survive a Danger" (near Hongmiaoling, the border to Zigui), there are quite a lot of stone carvings (including 16 Moya stone carvings, 8 stele carvings)

石刻（楚峡云开）　Stone Carving: Clouds Broken in Chu Strait

　　摩崖石刻或刻于陡峭的崖壁之上，或镌于独立的巨石之中，所处的海拔高度各不相等，刻字内容、字体各不相同。这些题刻，言简意赅，除个别为三、五言外，大都为四言形式，刻字一般为横书、阴刻、隶书，边有竖题小字署名作记。字体均苍劲有力，笔法如一，具有较高的书法艺术价值。题刻与其所在的地理位置，山川险境，水文航运有密切关系；或赞美长江两岸风光，如"灵山圣境"、"共话好江山"、"楚峡云开"；或因景生情，感慨万千，如"川流悟道"、"楚蜀鸿沟"、"要区天成"、"浪淘英雄"等，或叙述长江航运情景，如"孤舟渡"、"我示行周"、"化险为夷"等。还有一种石刻，刻于江边偏僻险要的羊肠山路旁，是劝戒打劫者勿做恶事，以善为本的，颇具教化含义，如刻在铜盆溪旁石壁上的"为善最乐"、"阿弥陀佛"。

石刻（楚峡云开的石联）

Some stone carvings were made in steep cliffs, or in gigantic stones, they are different in altitude, content and fonts. These carvings are mostly 4-word Chinese ancient poems, except a few 3-word, 5-words poems, horizontally aligned, chevets, in Li Font, with signature. All the calligraphies are rare art works, and the content concerns landscapes, hydrology and shipping; some describe landscape on both sides of Changjiang River, e.g. "Fairyland of Lingshan", "A Mutual Trip", "Clouds Broken in Chu Strait"; some release author's senses and thoughts, e.g. What the River says, Boundary Stone between Chu and Shu, Garrison set by God, Heroes survive Billows; some draw the pictures of shipping in the River, Canoe, I Point the Way, Survive a Danger. What's more, there is another kind of stone carving left on both mountain roads, especially some sermons, e.g. the carvings "Joy of Good Deeds", "Amitabha". Most carvings were made by ancient officials or literary masters, especially Qing Dynasty's Jingzhou Observer Li Ba, who contributed most works. The carvings record Three-Strait's sceneries and traffic, express the people's praise over Three-Strait. They play an important part in Three-Strait's history, culture and natural views, besides, occupying special position in the history.

徐光劢 楚峡云开

STONE CARVINGS OF WU STRAIT

　　是受了神女的挑逗，还是被巫峡的秀色所引诱？古往今来的文人墨客似乎对巫峡有着一种超乎寻常的迷恋。诗兴在这里发，墨迹在这里留，一幅幅石刻绵延不断，把个长长的巫峡布置成了一道石刻展厅。

　　那一幅幅石刻都称得上是艺术精品："我示行周"、"化险为夷"、"要区天成"、"灵山圣境"、"兀源仙泉"、"楚蜀鸿沟"、"楚峡云开"、"浪淘英雄"、"川流悟道"、"共话好山川"等等，看上去字迹刚劲，镌刻精细。从书写到镌刻都经过了巧妙的构思和认真的布局。每当我站在这些作品面前，便被一股强烈的艺术磁力吸引住了。于是放飞思绪，于是我行我素，穿越时空隧道去与那些文人墨客一个个会面，海阔天空地笑谈一气，借此风雅一回。

　　在巫峡北岸的一道石壁上，镌刻着"楚蜀鸿沟"四个大字。这里是湖北与四川交界之地，一幅石刻，便为两省划定了界线。遒劲的"楚蜀鸿沟"四个大字，引得古往今来的文人墨客密切关注，每每有诗赋于此。清光绪年间，四川荣县人赵熙金榜题名，赴京应试乘船路过此地，一眼看见"楚蜀鸿沟"四个字，感慨万千，当即赋诗一首：

Wu Strait has been a destination for scholars, are they attracted by the sexy goddess or scenic Wu Strait? They left numerous immortal poems on the stones, make the long Wu Strait a gallery of stone carvings.

Every stone carving is a classical artwork, e.g., I point the way, Survive a Danger, Garrison set by God, Fairyland of Lingshan, Spring of Wuyuan, Boundary Stone between Chu and Shu, Clouds Broken in Chu Strait, What the River says, A Mutual Trip, all carvings are attractive in calligraphy, fine in engraving. Both writing and engraving are elaborated. Every time I read these works, I always go back to the times when the authors lived, I talked with everyone of them, and feel as if I were a member of them.

Boundary Stone between Chu and Shu is a stone carving on north bank of Wu Strait, the border between Hubei and Sichuan. It has drawn attention of numerous scholars of all ages, and inspired them to contribute poems in here. In Guang Xu of Qing Dynasty, Zhao Xu, a

"共话好山川" 石刻　Stone Carving: A Mutual Trip

楚蜀此分疆，无狼亦断肠。

两山留缺口，一步即他乡。

此时此刻的赵熙，应该说是正值春风得意之时。可在离开家乡进入湖北的一刹那，心情蓦地起了变化。是啊，越过这条鸿沟，又是一方天地了。金榜题名对于他来说，是福还是祸，难以说清楚。这时的他一定是想起了李白的诗《蜀道难》，有了警觉。官场黑暗、险恶，处处暗藏杀机，那仕途如同崎岖狭窄的蜀道，艰险而难走哇！

与赵熙相反，文豪郭沫若看见这四个字则是另一种心态。一九六一年九月十六日，郭沫若游完重庆，乘坐"江泸"号轮顺江而下，行至巫峡看见"楚蜀鸿沟"四个字，顿时心潮澎湃，豪情满怀。直立船头赋诗一首：

群壑奔荆楚，一溪定界边。

船头已入鄂，船尾尚留川。

周超 "我示行周"石刻 Stone Carving: I point the way

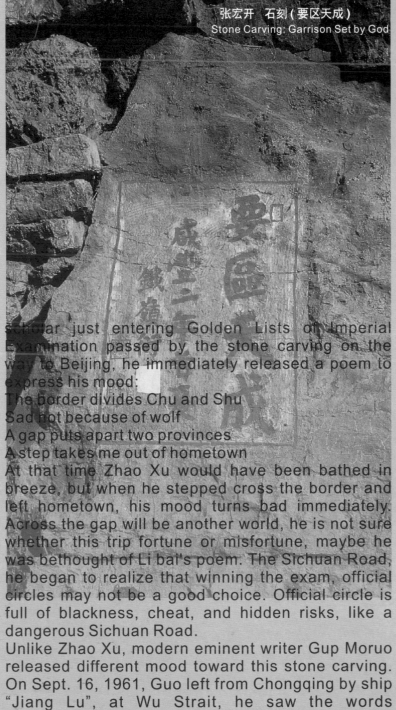

張宏开　石刻（要区天成）
Stone Carving: Garrison Set by God

scholar just entering Golden Lists of Imperial Examination passed by the stone carving on the way to Beijing, he immediately released a poem to express his mood:

The border divides Chu and Shu
Sad not because of wolf
A gap puts apart two provinces
A step takes me out of hometown

At that time Zhao Xu would have been bathed in breeze, but when he stepped cross the border and left hometown, his mood turns bad immediately. Across the gap will be another world, he is not sure whether this trip fortune or misfortune, maybe he was bethought of Li bai's poem. The Sichuan Road, he began to realize that winning the exam, official circles may not be a good choice. Official circle is full of blackness, cheat, and hidden risks, like a dangerous Sichuan Road.

Unlike Zhao Xu, modern eminent writer Gup Moruo released different mood toward this stone carving. On Sept. 16, 1961, Guo left from Chongqing by ship "Jiang Lu", at Wu Strait, he saw the words "Boundary Stone between Chu and Shu", he wrote the following poem:

All mountains crowd in Jing Chu
A brook borders two
Boat head enters Hubei province
Buttock remain in Shu

At that time, China enters a new age. The people holds a common aims, "all mountains run to Jingchu", everywhere takes on encouraging looks, Guo Moruo, like every citizen of new China, can't suppress the joy and expectation. At that moment, Guo might think of Li Bai's widely-known poems "one day all billows are broken, boat freely sails in the ocean". Stone Carving is a unique form of art, it has long life, winning love of knights of pen. In Qianlong of Qing Dynasty, there is a man fond of poems, his name is Li Ba. Li Ba wished his works seen by the world, he made many stone carvings in Wu Strait. Li Ba is observer of South Jingzhou, an official of irrigation works. According to legends, one day, on the tour of Three-strait irrigation works, it had been raining for days, so Li Ba felt depressed. However, unexpectedly, when the boat went out Wu Strait, sun went out suddenly, this made Li think of Kou Zhun, the famous prime minister of Song Dynasty, who ever acted as governor of Badong County for 3 years, he was honest, diligent, worried about people, under his leadership, the formerly poor Badong County was well developed in various industries, people's life was significantly improved, Kou

巴东老城　Badong Old City

张安立　灵山圣境（石刻）　Stone Carving: Fairyland of Lingshan

　　此时正值新中国建设的高潮时期，人们为着一个共同的目标"群鉴奔荆楚"，那万马奔腾的势头好不鼓舞人心，好不振奋人心！作为诗人郭沫若，也是其中建设者之一，那豪迈的情怀就自不待说了。我想这时的他也一定想起了李白的诗。不过不是《蜀道难》，而是李白那抒发豪情壮志的千古名句："乘风破浪会有时，直挂云帆济沧海。"石刻艺术表现手法独到，生命力强，因而被文人墨客看重。清乾隆年间有个叫李拔的人，所喜舞文弄墨。走到哪里，总要来上几笔，留个纪念什么的。一个巫峡，就有他的石刻多处。李拔何许人也？荆南观察使。在当时兼管水利。相传，李拔乘船巡视三峡水利顺江而下，一路上阴雨连绵，云遮雾障，心情十分郁闷。岂知，船一出巫峡口，天气突然由阴转晴，云开雾散。于是心情变好了，倏地想起了北宋名相寇准。寇准曾任过三年巴东知县。在任期间，勤政爱民，廉洁奉公。把个穷巴东治理得林茂粮丰，百业兴旺，人们吃不愁，穿不愁。百姓称他为"寇巴东"、"寇青天"。这天气突然变好，现出青天，难道是……想到此，李拔当即挥毫写下了"楚峡云开"四个大字，吩咐人立即刻在石壁上，以示对寇准的敬仰。

时间到了晚清，人们把李拔题的"楚峡云开"四个字看作了一幅对联的横批，由此引出了续联人。巴东县江北秀才吴骏绩，闲来游玩到此，看见"楚峡云开"四个字，不禁感慨万千。不假。寇准是良吏。但像寇准这样的良吏，古往今来实在是不多呀！于是，提笔写下了"历叹古今良吏少"上联，接下来写下联，却怎么也想不出来了，只好收笔作罢。这上联实在是难得对，难住了许许多多续联人。这一难就难了一百多年，直到民国六年，新任巴东知县冯锦文才续了下联。冯锦文是江西宜丰人，出身贫寒，心里时时装着穷苦百姓。哀民之艰，叹民之难，忧民之辛，思民之苦。看了吴骏绩"历叹古今良吏少"的上联，抑制不住内心激动，当即提笔写下了"须知天下苦人多"的下联。这幅对联，前后由三个人吟作，历经一百四十七年方才续成。说得上是一幅奇联。而且一反作对联先上联再下联后横批的常规，是先有横批，再有上联，后有下联。更是奇中称奇。因而这幅对联被人们十分看重。凡来巫峡观赏石刻的人，无不在这幅石刻前要多驻足一些时辰，凝目静思，品味再三。

was called "Kou Badong", "Judge Kou (Kou Qing Tian)". Now the weather changed so well unexpectedly, it must say thanks to Kou Qingtian, so he wrote the words "Clouds Broken in Chu Strait", in order to express worship toward Kou Zhun.

In late Qing Dynasty, the words "Clouds Broken in Chu Strait" was regarded as title the central line of a couplet, so there spreading more stories about author of the couplet. One day, Wu Junji, a Governmental Student of Badong County, saw the words "Clouds Broken in Chu Strait" in a roam, he said to himself, "Kouzhun is virtually a upright official in the history", so he wrote the first line of a couplet "why are there so few upright officials in the history?", but he couldn't get the second line for the couplet. So he left the first line alone, such a puzzle remained for over 100 years till the 6th year of the Republic of China, when Feng Wenjing, the new governor of Badong County completed the second line. Feng was born in a poor family in Yifeng, Jiangxi, he kept in mind the life of the people, worried about the people's hardship. By chance he saw the first line of Wu Junji, he put down "because there are so many poor people", such a couplet, made by three people of different ages, took 147 years. More interesting, it first completed the central line, then the first line, the second line, very seldom in works of Chinese couplet. As a result, such a couplet drew wide attention of numerous tourists, whoever see it will stand before it for a while, chew every word of every line.

I point the way is another stone carving on the south bank of Wu Strait. It is a square, 1m high, 4m long. It was inscribed by Tong Zetian in 1905 (Year 31, Guang Xu of Qing Dynasty). Tong Tianze, born in Chongqing, was member of Chuangjiang Irrigation Works Committee. I point the way, comes from the sentenced "Point Way for me", taken from Xiaoya, Deer's Voice, Book of Songs (Shi Jing), one of the seminal works of Chinese Civilization. The sentence was ever interpreted by Tang Moyao by quoting Yao Jiheng's General Essay "means pointing way for me", so here Tong Tianze wishes to point the way for the people, and to do something practical for the people. He made site survey over Wu Strait, collected detailed information of local topography and hydrology. To provide convenience to pedestrians and boatmen in traffic, he organized the people to build plank roads through the cliffs, when the works was completed, he made the stone "I point the way". The stone carving is not to record Tong's performance, he just wished to make a traffic mark, show to the people how to walk on the plank road when water rise. Later, as Tong expected, the stone became a sign guiding pedestrians. When water rises or falls, the people will refer to the stone carving, if the words go out of water, both

在巫峡口南岸的一道石壁上，镌刻着"我示行周"四个大字。这一幅石刻呈长方型，约有一米高，四米长。为光绪三十一年（1905年）童天泽题写。童天泽是重庆人。时任川江水利监修委员。"我示行周"一语，原出自《诗经》小雅·鹿鸣"示我周行"。童天泽在这里只是将四个字颠倒了一下位置。对这四个字，袁愈荌和唐莫尧先生编写的《诗经注》有专门解释。袁愈荌先生译"示我周行"为指我大路好方向，唐莫尧先生译时引用姚际恒《通论》释为"犹云指我路途耳"。童天泽将"示我周行"改为"我示行周"，便成为"我指大路好方向"、"我指路途了"。用时下的话说，童天泽还真是一个干实事的人。他深入巫峡作实地考察，详细掌握了这里的地势水情。为方便行人走路、船夫拉纤，组织民工凿壁修建栈道，完工后，便题写了"我示行周"四个大字。童天泽题写"我示行周"四个字，并非是要表现自己，为自己树碑立传。而是就此划一道警界线，告诉人们水涨水退栈道怎么个走法。这四个字还真成了过往行人的座标。峡江水涨水退，人们都盯着这四个字。四个字露出水面，行人行船只管过道；若四个字被水淹没，行人行船就得打驻。否则，便会大祸临头。"我示行周"四个字，还真是神奇！直到如今，人们出入巫峡仍以它为座标。由此，人们记住了童天泽。看见"我示行周"四个字，便想起了这位为民办实事的水利监修委员。

pedestrians and boat can continue their journey with ease, however, when the words are hidden in the water, both pedestrians and boats must stop. The stone let Tong Tianze occupy our memory, on seeing the carvings "I point way", we will remember the member of irrigation works committee.

Tong Tianze became a forever hero in the people's memory, because his carvings "I point the way" brought convenience to the people. This also makes some people jealous, such as Zhang Zhouyan, the governor of Badong county in Year 26 of Republic of China. Zhang, born in Dazhu, Sichuan and graduated from State Wusong Political University, would have been a learned scholars. He was ill-affected when reading Tong's carvings. "A plank road made such a hero, how easy it is!", said he to himself, "so can I". He immediately inscribed Heroes survive Billows on a place named Black Stone. It's true, there are countless heroes recorded in the history, but how many of them can survive billows? According to Zhang's carvings, Tong Tianze will be flushed away billows, only learned scholars like himself can survive billows. Unfortunately, no more than years later, the "hero surviving billows" was imprisoned, "flushed away by a billow", because he abolished bans of opium, squeezed the people, embezzled

童天泽为民办实事，修通栈道，方便了行人和拉纤的船夫，并刻下"我示行周"四个字警示人们，成了人们心目中的英雄。这样一来，自然有一些人看不顺眼。民国二十六年，巴东新上任一位县长。该县长姓张名胄炎，四川大竹人，国立吴淞政治大学毕业，可谓饱学之士。看了石刻"我示行周"四个字，心里颇不是滋味。修了条栈道，便成了人们心目中的英雄，这样的英雄得来也未免太容易了。于是提笔运腕，在巫峡北岸一地名叫黑石子的石壁上题写了"浪淘英雄"四个大字。是啊，古往今来的英雄知多少？有多少英雄经得起历史的大浪淘洗？这位张县长的话还真来得直截了当，童天泽这样的英雄是迟早要被浪淘掉的。那经得住几个浪头碰撞的英雄，非他这位饱学之士莫属。岂知，时隔短短两年，这位题写"浪淘英雄"的张县长就被浪淘掉了。张在任期间，废弛烟禁，搜刮民财，大肆侵吞屠宰税，案发后当即被撤职查办。那刻写在石壁上的"浪淘英雄"四个字，便成了历史笑柄。

butcher tax. The carvings Heroes Survive Billows naturally became a forever jest at his misdeeds.

Fortunately, there are not too many impudent men like Zhang Zhouyan. Near the carvings "Wuyuan Spring", "What the River says" is carved in a stone wall. The word "Told" is the "eye-drawing" part of this carving works. The life is a journey through a river, you must overcome the risks hidden in the shoals or reefs, every step forward may spend a lot of hardwork, nobody shall consider himself no ordinary being.

So we say Zhang Huanian, Liang Kaihua and Chen Wendian are such self-knowledge men, they three totally left a sentence "A Mutual Trip", which is carved on a stone on the south bank of Wu Strait, across Zhang Zhouyan's "Heroes Survive Billows", is seemingly jesting Zhang Zhouyan.

Carvings of Wuxia Strait, a recorder of Wu Strait's history, their ink have been exposed and polished by sunshine for hundreds of years, providing a heavy sense of history. Roaming in the gallery of stone carvings, every works is a meal of thoughts, what's more, it gives you a lot of psychology of life, as well as wisdom.

世上像张胃炎这样脸皮厚无自知之明的人，必定不多。离"兀源仙泉"石刻不远的一道石壁上，镌刻着"川流悟道"四个大字。这幅石刻作品，好就好在一个"悟"字！人生的路就像那滔滔峡江，三里一湾，五里一滩，处处有险阻。每前进一步，都是要付出艰辛的。哪能随随便便夸海口，自命不凡？

　　倒是那墨客张华年、梁开化、陈文典三人有自知之明，不敢轻易泼墨。天啦，那石刻是闹着玩儿的么？一旦刻上去就等于上了铜版册，想抹也抹不掉了。弄不好闹出笑话，会叫人一笑千年万年。三人结伴而行，逐幅品赏巫峡石刻，感触颇深，不论古，不说今，对巫峡的秀美风光各自发表一番感慨，最后共同写下五个字："共话好山川。"这幅石刻刻在巫峡南岸一个石头上，刚好与张胃炎的"浪淘英雄"对着面，隔江相望。让人看了颇有些犯疑，这是巧合，还是三人有意嘲弄张胃炎？不得而知。

　　巫峡石刻，以凝炼的文字记载了巫峡的过去。那些墨迹晾晒在太阳下，年复一年地烘烤，变得古陶一样釉黑发亮，显现出一种深沉的历史沧桑感。走进展厅，品赏每一幅作品，你不仅会得到一种美的享受，还会从中悟出一些做人的道理，由此变得聪明起来。

神农溪上的纤夫　　Trackers of Shen Nong Xi

神农溪漂流旅游示意图

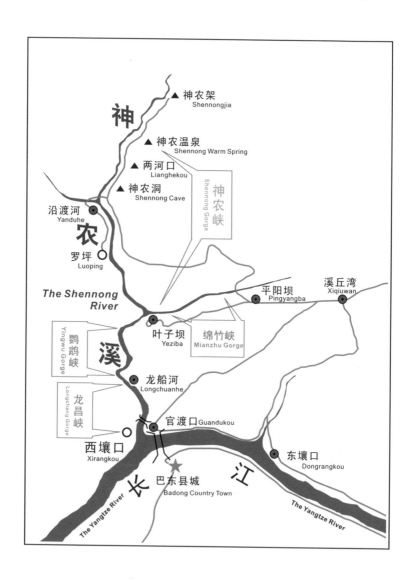

神

农

溪

▲ 神农架
Shennongjia

▲ 神农温泉
Shennong Warm Spring

▲ 两河口
Lianghekou

▲ 神农洞
Shennong Cave

神农峡
Shennong Gorge

沿渡河
Yanduhe

罗坪
Luoping

The Shennong River

鹦鹉峡
Yingwu Gorge

平阳坝
Pingyangba

溪丘湾
Xiqiuwan

叶子坝
Yeziba

绵竹峡
Mianzhu Gorge

龙船河
Longchuanhe

龙昌峡
Longchang Gorge

官渡口 Guandukou

西壤口
Xirangkou

东壤口
Dongrangkou

巴东县城
Badong Country Town

长 江
The Yangtze River

The Yangtze River

神农溪旅游线路及游览方式

Tour plan and methods to Shennong Stream

一、从巴东港乘观光游船进入神农溪，游览龙昌峡（悬棺、象鼻山、龙船河移民新村）、鹦鹉峡（高视岩、燕子阡大溶洞）、抵叶子坝后乘豌豆角扁舟感受古老的纤夫拉纤，观赏土家歌舞表演。乘船返回巴东港，结束愉快旅行，全程50KM，时间约4个半小时。

二、从巴东港乘观光游船进入神农溪，游览龙昌峡（悬棺、象鼻山、龙船河移民新村）、鹦鹉峡（高视岩、燕子阡大溶洞）、神农峡（石罅类岩棺、神农峰）；抵罗坪后乘豌豆角扁舟游览绵竹峡，乘船返回巴东港，结束愉快旅行。全程55KM，时间5个小时。

1.Start from badong port by tourist boat into shennong river, visiting longchang gorge (including ancient coffins, mt. Xiangbi (elephant-trunk), settlement village at longchuan he), yingwu (parrot) gorge (including gaoshi rock, yanziqian cave), arrive at yeziba, visiting mianzhu (soft bamboo) gorge, watching performance of tujia dance. Return to badong port by boat after a happy four-and-a-half-hour-journey of 50 km.

2.Start from badong port by tourist boat into shennong river, visiting longchang gorge (including ancient coffins, mr. Xiangbi (elephent-trunk), settlement village at longchuan he), yinwu (parrot) gorge (including gaoshi rock, yanziqian cave), shennong gorge (including stone coffins, shennong peak). Arrive at luoping, watching the performance of boat-tracking on peasecod boat, watching the performance of folk dance of tujia minority. Return to badong port by boat after a happy five-hour-journey of 55 km.

常规路线：
1、新三峡、神农溪、神农架 "双神" 游
2、宜昌、神农溪、白帝城、宜昌往返游
3、宜昌、神农溪、新三峡、重庆

1.Tour:New Three Gorges, tour of Two Shennong's (Shennong River, Shennong Jia)
2.Two-way Tour: Yichang - Shennong River - Bai-di (Emperor Bai) City - Yichang
3.Tour: Yichang - Shennong River - New Three Gorges - Chongqing

《神农溪上的纤夫》编辑部名单：

主　　编：周　超

摄　　影：周　超、张宏开、徐光宣、郑定荣、
　　　　　张安立、赵世华、邓　新　刘启明

撰　　文：戴箕忠、徐光宣、刘启明、钟秀林
　　　　　高源章　周　超